Would you believe it!

Wood

CATHERINE CHAMBERS

Evans

EVANS BROTHERS LIMITED

Evans Brothers Limited
2A Portman Mansions
Chiltern Street
London W1M 1LE

© Evans Brothers Limited 1995

Printed in Hong Kong by
Wing King Tong Co. Ltd

ISBN 0 237 51540 7

British Library Cataloguing in Publication Data.
A catalogue record for this book is available from the British Library.

Acknowledgements

Editor: Rachel Cooke
Designer: Neil Sayer
Production: Jenny Mulvanny
Photography: Michael Stannard
For permission to reproduce the following material the author and publishers gratefully acknowledge the following:
Cover (top right) Tim Shepherd/Oxford Scientific Films, (top left) Werner Forman Archive/National Museum of New Zealand, Wellington, (bottom right) Alan Becker/The Image Bank, (bottom left) Jane Legate/Robert Harding Picture Library, (logo insert, front and back) Chuck Place/The Image Bank **title page** (logo insert) Chuck Place/The Image Bank, (main picture) Christine Osborne Pictures **page 6** (top) William S. Paton/Bruce Coleman Limited, (bottom) Mark Hamblin/Oxford Scientific Films **page 7** (top) Sally Morgan/Ecoscene, (bottom) Erik Schaffer/Ecoscene **page 8** (top) Terry Middleton/Oxford Scientific Films, (bottom) Christine Osborne Pictures **page 9** (top) Terje Rakke/The Image Bank, (bottom) Simon Harris/ Robert Harding Picture Library **page 10** (left) K. A. Vollborn/The Image Bank, (right) Christine Osborne Pictures **page 11** (top) Werner Forman Archive/Courtesy Entwistle Gallery, London, (bottom) Werner Forman Archive/The Egyptian Museum, Cairo **page 12** (top) Werner Forman Archive/National Museum of New Zealand, Wellington, (bottom) Max Gibbs/ Oxford Scientific Films **page 13** (top) David W. Jones/Lakeland Life Picture Library, (bottom) Robert Harding Picture Library **page 14** (top) Michael Macintyre, The Hutchison Library, (bottom) Liba Taylor/The Hutchison Library **page 15** (top) The Hutchison Library, (bottom) David Bromwell/The Image Bank **page 16** (top) Liba Taylor/The Hutchison Library, (bottom) Werner Forman Archive/Musee Royale de l'Afrique Centrale, Tervuren **page 17** (top) Jane Legate/Robert Harding Picture Library, (bottom) Rick Rickman/The Image Bank **page 18** Sassoon/Robert Harding Picture Library **page 19** (top) Adam Woolfitt/Robert Harding Picture Library, (bottom) Christine Osborne Pictures **page 20** (top) Antlantide SDF/Bruce Coleman Limited, (bottom) Anthony King/Medimage **page 21** (top) The Hutchison Library, (bottom) Robert Harding Picture Library **page 22** (top) Werner Forman Archive/Museum fur Volkerkunde, (bottom) Sally Morgan/Ecoscene **page 23** (top) Bernard Regent/The Hutchison Library, (bottom) Schiller/Schuster/Robert Harding Picture Library **page 24** (top) Science Photo Library, (bottom) The Ronald Grant Archive **page 25** (top) Simon Tupper, Oxford Scientific Films, (bottom) Liba Taylor/The Hutchison Library **page 26** Dr Eckart Pott/Bruce Coleman Limited **page 27** (top) Werner Forman Archive/Canterbury Museum, Christchurch, (bottom) Sarah Errington/The Hutchison Library **page 28** (top) Adrian Morgan/ Bruce Coleman Limited

CONTENTS

What is wood?   **6**

Building with wood   **8**

Sitting on wood   **10**

Shaping wood   **12**

Wood on the move   **14**

Playing with wood   **16**

Wood and water   **18**

Musical wood   **20**

Writing on wood   **22**

Full of chemicals   **24**

Flaming wood   **26**

Find out for yourself   **28**

World map   **30**
   This map shows the places
   named in the book

Index   **30**

WHAT IS WOOD?

It is hard to believe that the hard, chunky wood of a tree trunk is made up of tiny tubes. These carry sap between the roots and the leaves. Sap is made up of water and minerals. This is the tree's food. But wood is not only important to a healthy tree. People use wood in many amazing ways, too.

Conifer trees
Scots pine trees belong to a group of trees called conifers. They have leaves like needles and woody cones. The wood from these trees is known as softwood.

How old is a tree?
All wood has markings called grain, which you see when a tree is cut down. In some trees the grain grows each year in two rings. You can count these to work out the tree's age.

Stringy palms

Palm trees like these Californian palms do not grow wood at all. Instead, their trunks are made up of stringy fibres. But some palm trunks are so hard, they are used like wood.

Flowering trees

Many trees, like this eucalyptus, have flowers rather than cones. Their leaves tend to be broad and flat. The wood from flowering trees is called hardwood.

BUILDING WITH WOOD

Wood is usually very tough. It can stay strong for a very long time. Wood has been used for buildings and supports for thousands of years.

Holding up rock
In this copper mine, a pile of rocks rests on a strong wooden support. Pine woods are often used as pit props and floors.

Crossing a bridge
The pathway of this long suspension bridge in Malaysia is built with wooden boards.

A tough frame

This wooden roof frame is being made in Norway. Here, thick snow weighs on houses in winter. The Norway spruce tree makes strong roof frames.

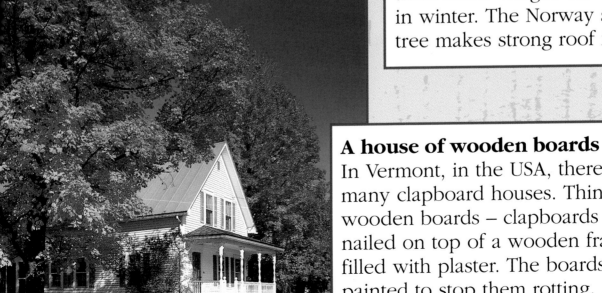

A house of wooden boards

In Vermont, in the USA, there are many clapboard houses. Thin wooden boards – clapboards – are nailed on top of a wooden frame filled with plaster. The boards are painted to stop them rotting.

SITTING ON WOOD

Wood can be cut or carved. It can be stuck or screwed together. So wood is good for making furniture, from chairs and tables to beds and cupboards, which can be longlasting and very beautiful.

Roomfuls of wood

Most of the furniture in these two rooms has been made of wood but it all looks very different. People can create a huge variety of furniture by using different types of wood, techniques and designs.

A sacred stool

In many parts of Africa, stools are carved out of a single piece of wood. This one was decorated with brass studs. It was made in Zaire. The way the carved woman sits shows she is thinking of people who have died.

Made to last

This wood and brass furniture is 4,500 years old! It shows how long wood can last. The bed and chair were found in the tomb of Queen Hetep-heres I at Giza, in Egypt.

SHAPING WOOD

Wood is tough, but it can also be carved or bent into all sorts of patterns and shapes.

A wooden mask

A Maori artist from New Zealand has shaped, patterned and pierced wood to make a mask. The patterns represent a real person's face, which other people will recognise.

A picture of wood

A carpenter from Thailand is using chisels, scrapers and knives to carve this picture panel. Panels like this are often made into chests.

Bending a basket
In the north of England, baskets are woven out of oak wood. The oak is split, boiled, and peeled into flexible strips. These are then woven into a hard-wearing basket.

A pestle and mortar
This wooden bowl, or mortar, has been carved out of one piece of strong wood. So has the thick wooden stick, or pestle. In West Africa, they are used to pound cereals and root crops, such as yams, before cooking them.

13

WOOD ON THE MOVE

Wood can be tough and heavy, or springy and light. From carts to aircraft, people have found these qualities very useful in getting them from place to place.

Skating on wood

In Los Angeles, USA, two skateboarders show off their tricks on springy wooden skateboards.

Wooden wheels

The whole of this cart in Romania is made out of wood. The first wheels were carved from wood thousands of years ago. They were round discs, joined to an axle with wooden pins. This type of wheel was very heavy, so later people cut out parts of the wheel, leaving spokes. This made the wheel lighter.

Water wheels

This water wheel in Syria is made of wood. Water runs in a channel beneath it and catches on the wheel's slats. This turns the wheel. And, as the wheel turns, it moves grinding stones inside the mill house. The stones crush cereals into flour.

Gliding on wood

Wooden wheels do not work so well on snow, but wood is still very useful for moving over snow and ice. People make sleds and skis of wood because it can be rubbed very smooth and glides swiftly over the snow.

PLAYING WITH WOOD

From the earliest times, people have found wood ideal for making toys and games.

Wooden chessmen
Chess boards and their carved pieces are used all over the world. These players are in Russia.

A carved car
This carved car was made as a gift for a child earlier this century in Zaire.

Bouncy bats!
Baseball bats like these need to be very springy, to hit the ball far. Springy bats also stop your wrists from hurting if you hit hard. Hockey sticks and cricket bats work in the same way.

Toys for toddlers
Wood can be carved into simple shapes, like this train. It is easily held by small hands. The wood is rubbed smooth, so it has no sharp edges, and painted bold, bright colours!

WOOD AND WATER

It's hard to believe that even heavy wood can float. But it's true! Rafts, canoes and sailing ships can be made out of wood. Wood can hold in water, too.

Floating homes
This fishing village is floating on the Langa River in Vietnam. The houses rest on wooden islands. Long poles stop them from floating away.

Barrels of drink

Wood can keep liquids in as well as out. This wine barrel is being made in France. Strips of oak are bent into shape and held with iron hoops. The oak wood also adds flavour to the wine.

From logs to sailing ships

People used logs as the first boats. The logs were hollowed out with fire.

Gradually boats became bigger and faster but people still used wood. This boat in Greece is made of wooden planks nailed to a wooden frame. Older boats used wooden pegs instead of nails.

MUSICAL WOOD

Wood is excellent for music making. Simply tapping a stick of wood gives a musical note. Using wood to make musical instruments helps give them a rich and beautiful sound.

Blowing a tune
In Greece, a short, hollow wooden flute makes high musical notes.

In Australia, the didgeridoo is a huge, long tube hollowed out by termites! Its size gives it a very low note.

Wood and strings
A Spanish musician plucks the strings of his wooden guitar. The wood makes the note echo, giving a strong, rich tone. Guitars were first brought to Spain from North Africa about 800 years ago.

Deafening drums!
These drums from Rwanda are carved from a single piece of hardwood trunk. Animal skin is stretched over the top. They make a deep, booming sound. They are very noisy.

Strings and bows
A violin is made out of 68 pieces of wood! It is played by pulling a wood and horse-hair bow across the strings.

WRITING ON WOOD

Most of the paper we use, including the pages of this book, is made from wood.

Words on boards

You don't need paper to write on! This wooden board is used by Hausa children in northern Nigeria. They learn how to write the teachings of the Islamic religion in Arabic script.

Pulping wood

In Canada, logs float towards the paper mill. Here, the wood is pulped by scraping off tiny wood fibres and mixing them with water. Pulp is also made by soaking wood chips in chemicals.

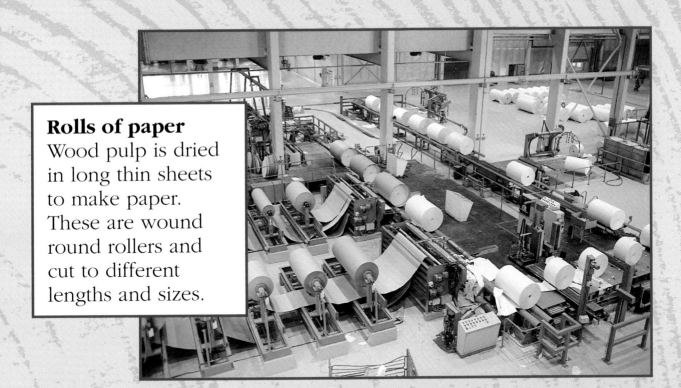

Rolls of paper

Wood pulp is dried in long thin sheets to make paper. These are wound round rollers and cut to different lengths and sizes.

Types of paper

Paper comes in all sorts of sizes, thicknesses, colours and patterns. The best quality paper gets pressed through rollers many times.

The first pulped paper was made out of bark nearly 2,000 years ago in China. Later, rags were used. Wood-pulp paper has only been made for about 160 years.

FULL OF CHEMICALS

Some woods contain useful chemicals. These are taken out of the wood to help make coloured dyes, glue, oils or even cattle food!

Sorting out the cellulose

Trees, like many plants, contain a chemical called cellulose. It forms in long chains, so tiny you can't see them. It is the cellulose in paper that helps it knit together. You can see the strands of cellulose in this close-up of lavatory paper.

Cellulose in the cinema!

Cellulose taken from wood has been used in making photographic and cinematic film. So wood helped film Charlie Chaplin! Cellulose has also helped to give shiny laquers and soft materials such as rayon and viscose.

Healthy cattle

Farm animals and chickens need vitamins in their food to keep them healthy. Yeast is often added to their feed. This has got vitamin B in it. The yeast can be made with the help of lignin, a chemical taken out of wood.

Chewing on wood

Wood can be good for your teeth! These young men in Bangladesh are brushing their teeth with chew sticks. The sticks are as good as toothbrushes. They are taken from trees with cleaning chemicals in them. Chewing on the sticks releases the chemicals, which clean the teeth.

FLAMING WOOD

Wood makes a good fire. But when wood is burned very slowly in a pit, charcoal is made. You can cook over charcoal, or draw with it.

A wood pile

In Germany, a woman builds a wood kiln to make charcoal. The wood is packed tight so that it burns slowly. Too much air makes it burn too fast, leaving ashes instead of charcoal.

Smoking wood

The pile of wood is covered with grass and set alight. Extra grass has to be raked often over the fire. The pile burns for a few days, slowly turning the wood to charcoal.

Charcoal art

These charcoal drawings were done by Maori artists in New Zealand about 600 years ago. They show birds, a fish and a man. Artists still use charcoal. Willow and spindle-wood charcoal are good for drawing.

Wood keeps you warm

In the Sudan, a pile of wood is carried back home. It will be burnt for cooking and to keep warm at night.

People have used wood as fuel from ancient times. But today in some places wood is running short. We must look after wood. Many people in Africa now use a special stove which uses less fuel.

FIND OUT FOR YOURSELF

Wood can be used in so many ways. Find out more about it for yourself. Here are some ideas to get you started.

Woodland watch

Trees and woodland are very precious to us today. How can you help to make the most of woodlands?

• Join a local conservation group or contact a forest development company. Your library should have details.

• Consider areas nearby you that could be planted with new trees. Even in cities, there are small patches of land that would make good woodland. Put together a project suggesting why the area should be planted. Think about these questions:

1. Will the new woodland spoil the lives of people living near it in any way? For example, will it block a beautiful view?

2. Can the woodland fit in with other activities in the area? Think about work, play and education in your area.

3. Will the woodland spoil the area for other wildlife?

4. What kinds of trees will grow on the land? Is it wet or dry? Is it flat or sloping? What kind of soil does it have? These conditions will affect your choice of tree.

5. Finally, will your woodland attract people to it?

If you think your case is good, find out how you could put your plans into action.

A woody collage

This picture has been made up of lots of different things connected with wood – twigs, sawdust, paper and cardboard. Collect together scraps of wood and wood products and make your own woody collage.

Drawing with wood

Try drawing with soft charcoal sticks – you can buy them from any art shop. See how many different effects you can get from fine lines to smudged shadows. The charcoal will make your hands dirty, though, so wash them when you've finished.

29

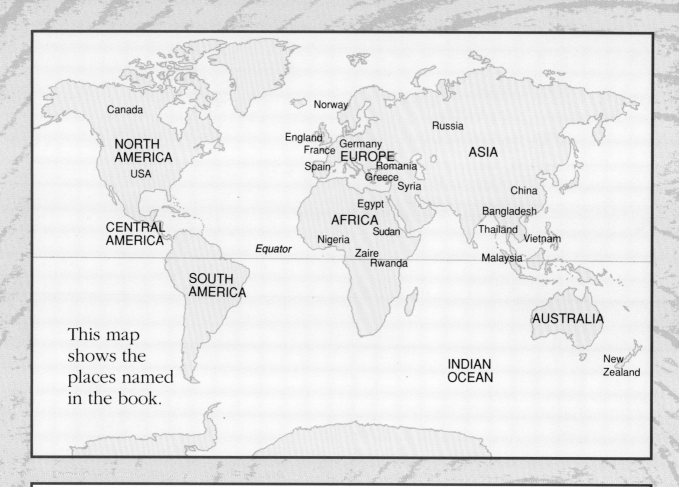

This map shows the places named in the book.

INDEX

animal feed 24, 25

barrel 19
baseball bat 17
basket 13
boat 18, 19
bridge 8

Californian palm 7
cellulose 24
charcoal 26-27
chess 16
chewing stick 25

clapboard 9
cricket bat 17

didgeridoo 20
drum 21
dye 24

eucalyptus 7

film 24
flute 20
furniture 10-11

glue 24
guitar 20

hockey stick 17
house 9, 18

lacquer 24

mask 12
material 24

Norway spruce tree 9

oak 13, 19

palm tree 7
panel 12
paper 22-23, 24

pestle and mortar 13
pit prop 8

roof 9

Scots pine tree 6
skateboard 14
skis and sleds 15
spindle-wood 27

violin 21
vitamin 25

wheel 14-15
willow tree 27